THE LITTLE BOOK OF
SELF-CARE
— FOR —
PISCES

*Simple Ways to Refresh
and Restore—According
to the Stars*

CONSTANCE STELLAS

ADAMS MEDIA

NEW YORK LONDON TORONTO SYDNEY NEW DELHI

Adamsmedia

Adams Media
An Imprint of Simon & Schuster, Inc.
100 Technology Center Drive
Stoughton, MA 02072

First Adams Media hardcover edition January 2019

ADAMS MEDIA and colophon are trademarks of Simon & Schuster.

For information about special discounts for bulk purchases,
please contact Simon & Schuster Special Sales at 1-866-506-1949 or
business@simonandschuster.com.

The Simon & Schuster Speakers Bureau can bring authors to your live event. For
more information or to book an event contact the Simon & Schuster Speakers
Bureau at 1-866-248-3049 or visit our website at www.simonspeakers.com.

Interior design by Colleen Cunningham
Interior images © Getty Images; Clipart.com

Manufactured in China

10 9 8

Library of Congress Cataloging-in-Publication Data has been applied for.

ISBN 978-1-5072-0986-8
ISBN 978-1-5072-0987-5 (ebook)

Dedication

To my intuitive, creative Pisces sister, Patti, with love.

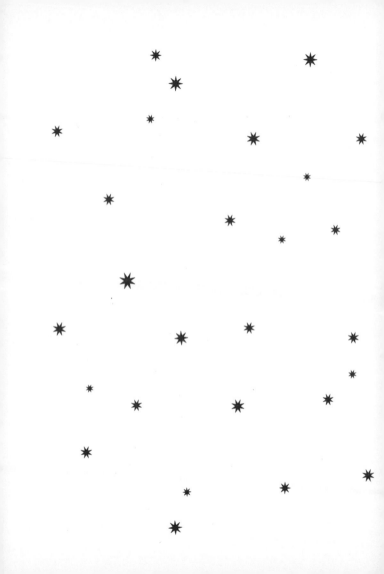

CONTENTS

Acknowledgments

I would like to thank Karen Cooper and everyone at Adams Media who helped with this book. To Brendan O'Neill, Katie Corcoran Lytle, Sarah Doughty, Eileen Mullan, Brett Palana-Shanahan, Casey Ebert, Sylvia Davis, and everyone else who worked on the manuscripts. To Frank Rivera, Colleen Cunningham, and Katrina Machado for their work on the book's cover and interior design. I appreciated your team spirit and eagerness to dive into the riches of astrology.

Introduction

It's time for you to have a little *"me" time*—powered by the zodiac. By tapping into your Sun sign's astrological and elemental energies, *The Little Book of Self-Care for Pisces* brings star-powered strength and cosmic relief to your life with self-care guidance tailored specifically for you.

While you may have a deep sense of community, Pisces, this book focuses on your true self. This book provides information on how to incorporate self-care into your life while teaching you just how important astrology is to your overall self-care routine. You'll learn more about yourself as you learn about your sign and its governing element, water. Then you can relax, rejuvenate, and stay balanced with more than one hundred self-care ideas and activities perfect for your Pisces personality.

From savoring a home-cooked meal to creating a personal altar, you will find plenty of ways to heal your mind, body, and active spirit. Now, let the stars be your self-care guide!

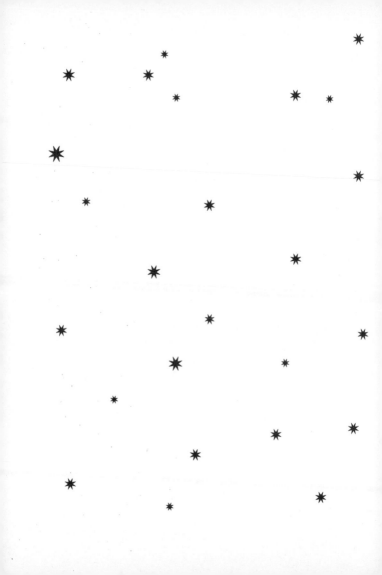

PART 1

SIGNS, ELEMENTS, ___ AND ___ SELF-CARE

CHAPTER 1
WHAT IS SELF-CARE?

✴

Astrology gives insights into whom to love, when to charge forward into new beginnings, and how to succeed in whatever you put your mind to. When paired with self-care, astrology can also help you relax and reclaim that part of yourself that tends to get lost in the bustle of the day. In this chapter you'll learn what self-care is—for you. (No matter your sign, self-care is more than just lit candles and quiet reflection, though these activities may certainly help you find the renewal that you seek.) You'll also learn how making a priority of personalized self-care activities can benefit you in ways you may not even have thought of. Whether you're a Leo, a Pisces, or a Taurus, you deserve rejuvenation and renewal that's customized to your sign—this chapter reveals where to begin.

What Self-Care Is

Self-care is any activity that you do to take care of yourself. It rejuvenates your body, refreshes your mind, or realigns your spirit. It relaxes and refuels you. It gets you ready for a new day or a fresh start. It's the practices, rituals, and meaningful activities that you do, just for you, that help you feel safe, grounded, happy, and fulfilled.

The activities that qualify as self-care are amazingly unique and personalized to who you are, what you like, and, in large part, what your astrological sign is. If you're asking questions about what self-care practices are best for those ruled by water and born under the sensitive eye of Pisces, you'll find answers—and restoration—in Part 2. But, no matter which of those self-care activities speak to you and your unique place in the universe on any given day, it will fall into one of the following self-care categories—each of which pertains to a different aspect of your life:

* Physical self-care
* Emotional self-care
* Social self-care
* Mental self-care
* Spiritual self-care
* Practical self-care

When you practice all of these unique types of self-care—and prioritize your practice to ensure you are choosing the best options for your unique sign and governing element—know that you are actively working to create the version of yourself that the universe intends you to be.

Physical Self-Care

When you practice physical self-care, you make the decision to look after and restore the one physical body that has been bestowed upon you. Care for it. Use it in the best way you can imagine, for that is what the universe wishes you to do. You can't light the world on fire or move mountains if you're not doing everything you can to take care of your physical health.

Emotional Self-Care

Emotional self-care is when you take the time to acknowledge and care for your inner self, your emotional well-being. Whether you're angry or frustrated, happy or joyful, or somewhere in between, emotional self-care happens when you choose to sit with your emotions: when you step away from the noise of daily life that often drowns out or tamps down your authentic self. Emotional self-care lets you see your inner you as the cosmos intend. Once you identify your true emotions, you can either accept them and continue to move forward on your journey or you can try to change any negative emotions for the better. The more you acknowledge your feelings and practice emotional self-care, the more you'll feel the positivity that the universe and your life holds for you.

Social Self-Care

You practice social self-care when you nurture your relationships with others, be they friends, coworkers, or family members. In today's hectic world it's easy to let relationships fall to the wayside, but it's so important to share your life with others—and let others share their lives with you. Social self-care is reciprocal and often karmic. The support and love that you put out into the universe through social self-care is given back to you by those you socialize with—often tenfold.

Mental Self-Care

Mental self-care is anything that keeps your mind working quickly and critically. It helps you cut through the fog of the day, week, or year and ensures that your quick wit and sharp mind are intact and working the way the cosmos intended. Making sure your mind is fit helps you problem-solve, decreases stress since you're not feeling overwhelmed, and keeps you feeling on top of your mental game—no matter your sign or your situation.

Spiritual Self-Care

Spiritual self-care is self-care that allows you to tap into your soul and the soul of the universe and uncover its secrets. Rather than focusing on a particular religion or set of religious beliefs, these types of self-care activities reconnect you with a higher power: the sense that something out there is bigger than you. When you meditate, you connect. When you pray, you connect. Whenever you do something that allows you to experience and marry yourself to the vastness that is the cosmos, you practice spiritual self-care.

Practical Self-Care

Self-care is what you do to take care of yourself, and practical self-care, while not as expansive as the other types, is made up of the seemingly small day-to-day tasks that bring you peace and accomplishment. These practical self-care rituals are important, but are often overlooked. Scheduling a doctor's appointment that you've been putting off is practical self-care. Getting your hair cut is practical self-care. Anything you can check off your list of things to be accomplished gives you a sacred space to breathe and allows the universe more room to bring a beautiful sense of cosmic fulfillment your way.

What Self-Care Isn't

Self-care is restorative. Self-care is clarifying. Self-care is whatever you need to do to make yourself feel secure in the universe.

Now that you know what self-care is, it's also important that you're able to see what self-care isn't. Self-care is not something that you force yourself to do because you think it will be good for you. Some signs are energy in motion and sitting still goes against their place in the universe. Those signs won't feel refreshed by lying in a hammock or sitting down to meditate. Other signs aren't able to ground themselves unless they've found a self-care practice that protects their cosmic need for peace and quiet. Those signs won't find parties, concerts, and loud venues soothing or satisfying. If a certain ritual doesn't bring you peace, clarity, or satisfaction, then it's not right for your sign and you should find something that speaks to you more clearly.

There's a difference though between not finding satisfaction in a ritual that you've tried and not wanting to try a self-care activity because you're tired or stuck in a comfort zone. Sometimes going to the gym or meeting up with friends is the self-care practice that you need to experience—whether engaging in it feels like a downer or not. So consider how you feel when you're actually doing the activity. If it feels invigorating to get on the treadmill or you feel delight when you actually catch up with your friend, the ritual is doing what it should be doing and clearing space for you—among other benefits...

The Benefits of Self-Care

The benefits of self-care are boundless and there's none that's superior to helping you put rituals in place to feel more at home in your body, in your spirit, and in your unique home in the cosmos. There are, however, other benefits to engaging in the practice of self-care that you should know.

Rejuvenates Your Immune System

No matter which rituals are designated for you by the stars, your sign, and its governing element, self-care helps both your body and mind rest, relax, and recuperate. The practice of self-care activates the parasympathetic nervous system (often called the rest and digest system), which slows your heart rate, calms the body, and overall helps your body relax and release tension. This act of decompression gives your body the space it needs to build up and strengthen your immune system, which protects you from illness.

Helps You Reconnect—with Yourself

When you practice the ritual of self-care—especially when you customize this practice based on your personal sign and governing element—you learn what you like to do and what you need to do to replenish yourself. Knowing yourself better, and allowing yourself the time and space that you need to focus on your personal needs and desires, gives you the gifts of self-confidence and self-knowledge. Setting time aside to focus on your needs also helps you put busy, must-do things aside, which gives you time to reconnect with yourself and who you are deep inside.

Increases Compassion

Perhaps one of the most important benefits of creating a self-care ritual is that, by focusing on yourself, you become more compassionate to others as well. When you truly take the time to care for yourself and make yourself and your importance in the universe a priority in your own life, you're then able to care for others and see their needs and desires in a new way. You can't pour from an empty dipper, and self-care allows you the space and clarity to do what you can to send compassion out into the world.

Starting a Self-Care Routine

Self-care should be treated as a ritual in your life, something you make the time to pause for, no matter what. You are important. You deserve rejuvenation and a sense of relaxation. You need to open your soul to the gifts that the universe is giving you, and self-care provides you with a way to ensure you're ready to receive those gifts. To begin a self-care routine, start by making yourself the priority. Do the customized rituals in Part 2 with intention, knowing the universe has already given them to you, by virtue of your sign and your governing element.

Now that you understand the role that self-care will hold in your life, let's take a closer look at the connection between self-care and astrology.

CHAPTER 2

SELF-CARE
AND ASTROLOGY

✳

Astrology is the study of the connection between the objects in the heavens (the planets, the stars) and what happens here on earth. Just as the movements of the planets and other heavenly bodies influence the ebb and flow of the tides, so do they influence you—your body, your mind, your spirit. This relationship is ever present and is never more important—or personal—than when viewed through the lens of self-care.

In this chapter you'll learn how the locations of these celestial bodies at the time of your birth affect you and define the self-care activities that will speak directly to you as a Leo, an Aries, a Capricorn, or any of the other zodiac signs. You'll see how the zodiac influences every part of your being and why ignoring its lessons can leave you feeling frustrated and unfulfilled. You'll also realize that, when you perform the rituals of self-care based on your sign, the wisdom of the cosmos will lead you down a path of fulfillment and restoration—to the return of who you really are, deep inside.

Zodiac Polarities

In astrology, all signs are mirrored by other signs that are on the opposite side of the zodiac. This polarity ensures that the zodiac is balanced and continues to flow with an unbreakable, even stream of energy. There are two different polarities in the zodiac and each is called by a number of different names:

* Yang/masculine/positive polarity
* Yin/feminine/negative polarity

Each polar opposite embodies a number of opposing traits, qualities, and attributes that will influence which self-care practices will work for or against your sign and your own personal sense of cosmic balance.

Yang

Whether male or female, those who fall under yang, or masculine, signs are extroverted and radiate their energy outward. They are spontaneous, active, bold, and fearless. They move forward in life with the desire to enjoy everything the world has to offer to them, and they work hard to transfer their inspiration and positivity to others so that those individuals may experience the same gifts that the universe offers them. All signs governed by the fire and air elements are yang and hold the potential for these dominant qualities. We will refer to them with masculine pronouns. These signs are:

* Aries
* Leo
* Sagittarius
* Gemini
* Libra
* Aquarius

There are people who hold yang energy who are introverted and retiring. However, by practicing self-care that is customized for your sign and understanding the potential ways to use your energy, you can find a way—perhaps one that's unique to you—to claim your native buoyancy and dominance and engage with the path that the universe opens for you.

Yin

Whether male or female, those who fall under yin, or feminine, signs are introverted and radiate inwardly. They draw people and experiences to them rather than seeking people and experiences in an extroverted way. They move forward in life with an energy that is reflective, receptive, and focused on communication and achieving shared goals. All signs governed by the earth and water elements are yin and hold the potential for these reflective qualities. We will refer to them with feminine pronouns. These signs are:

* Taurus
* Virgo
* Capricorn
* Cancer
* Scorpio
* Pisces

As there are people with yang energy who are introverted and retiring, there are also people with yin energy who are outgoing and extroverted. And by practicing self-care rituals that speak to your particular sign, energy, and governing body, you will reveal your true self and the balance of energy will be maintained.

Governing Elements

Each astrological sign has a governing element that defines their energy orientation and influences both the way the sign moves through the universe and relates to self-care. The elements are fire, earth, air, and water. All the signs in each element share certain characteristics, along with having their own sign-specific qualities:

* **Fire:** Fire signs are adventurous, bold, and energetic. They enjoy the heat and warm environments and look to the sun and fire as a means to recharge their depleted batteries. They're competitive, outgoing, and passionate. The fire signs are Aries, Leo, and Sagittarius.
* **Earth:** Earth signs all share a common love and tendency toward a practical, material, sensual, and economic orientation. The earth signs are Taurus, Virgo, and Capricorn.
* **Air:** Air is the most ephemeral element and those born under this element are thinkers, innovators, and communicators. The air signs are Gemini, Libra, and Aquarius.
* **Water:** Water signs are instinctual, compassionate, sensitive, and emotional. The water signs are Cancer, Scorpio, and Pisces.

Chapter 3 teaches you all about the ways your specific governing element influences and drives your connection to your cosmically harmonious self-care rituals, but it's important that you realize how important these elemental traits are to your self-care practice and to the activities that will help restore and reveal your true self.

Sign Qualities

Each of the astrological elements governs three signs. Each of these three signs is also given its own quality or mode, which corresponds to a different part of each season: the beginning, the middle, or the end.

* **Cardinal signs:** The cardinal signs initiate and lead in each season. Like something that is just starting out, they are actionable, enterprising, and assertive, and are born leaders. The cardinal signs are Aries, Cancer, Libra, and Capricorn.
* **Fixed signs:** The fixed signs come into play when the season is well established. They are definite, consistent, reliable, motivated by principles, and powerfully stubborn. The fixed signs are Taurus, Leo, Scorpio, and Aquarius.
* **Mutable signs:** The mutable signs come to the forefront when the seasons are changing. They are part of one season, but also part of the next. They are adaptable, versatile, and flexible. The mutable signs are Gemini, Virgo, Sagittarius, and Pisces.

Each of these qualities tells you a lot about yourself and who you are. They also give you invaluable information about the types of self-care rituals that your sign will find the most intuitive and helpful.

Ruling Planets

In addition to qualities and elements, each specific sign is ruled by a particular planet that lends its personality to those born under that sign. Again, these sign-specific traits give you valuable insight into the personality of the signs and the self-care rituals that may best rejuvenate them. The signs that correspond to each planet—and the ways that those planetary influences determine your self-care options—are as follows:

* **Aries:** Ruled by Mars, Aries is passionate, energetic, and determined.
* **Taurus:** Ruled by Venus, Taurus is sensual, romantic, and fertile.
* **Gemini:** Ruled by Mercury, Gemini is intellectual, changeable, and talkative.
* **Cancer:** Ruled by the Moon, Cancer is nostalgic, emotional, and home loving.
* **Leo:** Ruled by the Sun, Leo is fiery, dramatic, and confident.
* **Virgo:** Ruled by Mercury, Virgo is intellectual, analytical, and responsive.
* **Libra:** Ruled by Venus, Libra is beautiful, romantic, and graceful.
* **Scorpio:** Ruled by Mars and Pluto, Scorpio is intense, powerful, and magnetic.
* **Sagittarius:** Ruled by Jupiter, Sagittarius is optimistic, boundless, and larger than life.

* **Capricorn:** Ruled by Saturn, Capricorn is wise, patient, and disciplined.
* **Aquarius:** Ruled by Uranus, Aquarius is independent, unique, and eccentric.
* **Pisces:** Ruled by Neptune and Jupiter, Pisces is dreamy, sympathetic, and idealistic.

A Word on Sun Signs

When someone is a Leo, Aries, Sagittarius, or any of the other zodiac signs, it means that the sun was positioned in this constellation in the heavens when they were born. Your Sun sign is a dominant factor in defining your personality, your best self-care practices, and your soul nature. Every person also has the position of the Moon, Mercury, Venus, Mars, Jupiter, Saturn, Uranus, Neptune, and Pluto. These planets can be in any of the elements: fire signs, earth signs, air signs, or water signs. If you have your entire chart calculated by an astrologer or on an Internet site, you can see the whole picture and learn about all your elements. Someone born under Leo with many signs in another element will not be as concentrated in the fire element as someone with five or six planets in Leo. Someone born in Pisces with many signs in another element will not be as concentrated in the water element as someone with five or six planets in Pisces. And so on. Astrology is a complex system and has many shades of meaning. For our purposes looking at the self-care practices designated by your Sun sign, or what most people consider *their* sign, will give you the information you need to move forward and find fulfillment and restoration.

CHAPTER 3

ESSENTIAL ELEMENTS: WATER

✳

Water is the fourth and final element of creation. It is essential for the planet and for our physical existence. It is amorphous, meaning it assumes the shape of its container or geographical location and solidifies only when frozen. Those who have water as their governing element—Cancer, Scorpio, and Pisces—all have a special energy signature and connection with water that guides all aspects of their lives. Water signs are intuitive and tend to live on waves of feeling. They are reflective, responsive, and fertile, and are often more sensitive than other signs. Their path in life is to quell their overwhelming emotions and use their instincts for love and compassion toward themselves and others.

Their approach to self-care must include these goals. Let's take a look at the mythological importance of water and its fluid counterparts, the basic characteristics of the three water signs, and what they all have in common when it comes to self-care.

The Mythology of Water

In Greek mythology water is linked to the god of the sea, Poseidon. Poseidon was brother to Zeus and Hades, and one of the six children conceived by Rhea and Cronos. His father, Cronos, ruled the universe, but was eventually overthrown by Zeus. After their father's collapse of power, Zeus, Hades, and Poseidon decided to divide the earth between the three of them. Poseidon became the lord of the sea, while Zeus became lord of Mount Olympus and sky, and Hades became the lord of the underworld.

The sea god was especially important in the ancient world as sea travel and navigation formed the principal trade and travel routes. Throughout mythology, going to sea was seen as a precarious adventure, and sailors often prayed to Poseidon for safe return and calm waters. Many myths feature Poseidon saving a ship at the last moment. In other myths he is not so merciful.

Like Poseidon, water signs make their decisions based off emotion. Their gut feelings guide them. This makes water signs highly compassionate and understanding, but it can also make them moody at times. Water signs may try to keep their emotions balanced in the hope of staying in control of their feelings, rather than allowing their feelings to control them. This desire drives their likes and dislikes, personality traits, and approaches to self-care.

The Element of Water

In terms of astrology, the water signs are called the feeling signs. They feel first, and think and speak later. They are very familiar with the emotional expression of tears, laughter, anger, joy, and grief. They often wear their heart on their sleeve and are extremely sentimental. Scorpio is somewhat of an exception to this characterization, but, nevertheless, she has a sensitive feeling mechanism. A water sign's energy moves inward, and they draw people and experiences to them rather than overtly seeking out people and experiences. For example, Scorpio's bravery means she is always open to new adventures. Cancer's loyalty encourages her to stick close to family and friends. And Pisces's creative intuition makes her a wonderful problem-solver when faced with a difficult conundrum.

Astrological Symbols

The astrological symbols (also called the zodiacal symbols) of the water signs also give you hints as to how the water signs move through the world. The symbols of all the water signs are creatures connected with the sea, the cradle of life:

* Scorpio is the Scorpion (and the Eagle and the Phoenix)
* Cancer is the Crab
* Pisces is the two Fish tied together

Scorpio has a complex set of symbols because there are varieties of scorpions, both in the sea and on land, but the sea is home to all these sensitive water signs. Scorpio uses her stinger to sting first rather than take the time to ask questions. Cancer the Crab holds on to her home tenaciously and never approaches anything directly. Instead, she moves from side to side to go forward in zigzag motions. And Pisces's two Fish tied together symbolize duality—one of the fish staying above the water, paying attention to the earth, and the other living in the sea, where dreams and the imagination rule.

Signs and Seasonal Modes

Each of the elements in astrology also has a sign that corresponds to a different part of each season.

* **Cardinal:** Cancer, as the first water sign, comes at the summer solstice, when summer begins. She is a cardinal sign and the leader of the water signs. She may lead indirectly, but has a powerful desire to be in control.
* **Fixed:** Scorpio, the next water sign, is a fixed water sign, and she rules when autumn is well established. The fixed signs are definite, motivated by principles, and powerfully stubborn.
* **Mutable:** And Pisces, the last water sign and the last sign of the zodiac, is a mutable sign. She moves us from winter to the spring equinox in Aries. The major characteristic of mutable, or changeable, signs is flexibility.

If you know your element and whether you are a cardinal, fixed, or mutable sign, you know a lot about yourself. This is invaluable for self-care and is reflected in the customized water sign self-care rituals found in Part 2.

Water Signs and Self-Care

Self-care comes naturally to water signs. Oftentimes, they find it is essential to take care of themselves because they feel acutely when something is askew inside them. They may complain bitterly about not feeling well, or about their sensitivities or the weather, but they generally know what to do to get back on course. Physical self-care is the hardest area for the water signs to master, because they do not like to do things unless they feel like doing them. Once they have a routine that has proven will make them feel better, they will stick to it, but before they adopt that routine, they are often hit-or-miss when it comes to diet, exercise, and medical checkups. Water signs are also very in tune with alternative cures and what their ancestors did for self-care.

Another essential factor in water sign self-care is the atmosphere of the gym or exercise location. Generally, water signs do not like crowds. If it is 5 p.m. and people are pounding out their aggressions from work on the treadmill, most water signs will choose to wait for the crowds to thin, or go earlier in the day. However, one of the great encouragements for water signs is the use of a shower or pool—a water source that they can include in their routine is a great enticement for water signs. Water signs may choose to attend classes at the gym, but most of the time they prefer to make sure that they are not overly influenced by other people's vibes.

Water signs are especially drawn to natural surroundings when it comes to self-care. Walking by a pond or lake is perhaps the best exercise for them, as it combines physical, mental, and spiritual practice. In a low-pressure environment, water signs feel that all their activities are worthwhile, both in terms of money and time. They are very aware of the money they spend and tend to be prudent and almost stingy with funds. And there is a direct relationship between their feeling of well-being and how much money they have in the bank.

Water signs are nurturers and make it a priority to take care of family and friends. It is always best for water signs to frame their self-care in terms of their familial feelings about something. For example, the statement "If you quit eating all this junk, you will help your family by setting a good example and you will feel better" is a winning one for water signs, marrying their love for their family with their own self-care. Once the water sign gets the feeling that they can extend the love and care of their family to themselves through self-care, they feel more comfortable designating attention to wellness practices.

In terms of emotional self-care, the most important factor for water signs is to avoid exaggerating their reactions to events or people. The more water signs can stay in the here and now, the less they will feel there are imaginary scenarios of people working against them. They are so sensitive that it is very easy for them to lapse into being self-conscious. A very good technique for water signs is to play a game asking themselves the question, "How would I feel if I were that person?" This thinking pattern encourages compassion rather than self-centeredness in water signs.

Water signs have a gift for feeling. In today's society we tend to diminish the importance of being emotional. Water signs may feel they have to do all the heavy lifting in the emotional department, which may make them feel lonely. Water signs are naturally empathetic, so the trick for them is to balance how they feel about other people and extend those good feelings to themselves. Feelings are different from intellectual, inspirational, and practical concerns. The water signs symbolize the potential of members of the human family to share their individual feelings.

So, now that you know what water signs need to practice self-care, let's look at each of the characteristics of Pisces and how she can maintain her gifts.

CHAPTER 4

SELF-CARE FOR PISCES

✴

Dates: February 19–March 20
Element: Water
Polarity: Yin
Quality: Mutable
Symbol: Fish
Ruler: Neptune, Jupiter

Pisces is the last water sign and the twelfth and final sign of the zodiac. She is a mutable sign, ushering in the spring season. In astrology it is said that Pisces marks the end of the individual personality and the beginning of the return to spirit. The intangible, feeling world is Pisces's home, rather than the everyday material world. She is sensitive and psychically tuned in, seesawing between compassionate care for others and the tendency to always have her head in the clouds.

Pisces is one of the most spiritual signs. Her symbol is the two Fish tied together, and in many depictions one fish is above the water and in the light of day, while the other is under the sea and in darkness. Pisces's imagination and artistic abilities come from these underwater depths. Emotional sensitivity is the hallmark of all water signs, but in Pisces it is especially acute. Pisces needs more rest and downtime than other signs do. Reality is often too abrasive, and she needs to recoup her energies often to stay happy and balanced.

In ancient times when astrologers first began observing the stars, there were only seven planets visible but twelve zodiac constellations. At that time Pisces was ruled by Jupiter, who is also Sagittarius's ruler. Jupiter is called the Greater Benefic, and both Pisces and Sagittarius are blessed by his protection. The bountiful generosity of Jupiter and the desire to help humanity is part of the Piscean nature. In 1846 the planet Neptune was discovered, and after observation, astrologers assigned this misty planet as Pisces's second ruler. Mist is a good metaphor for Pisces, who enjoys an inner world where there is a constant pink haze of emotion and creativity.

Neptune is also a planet that symbolizes spiritual hopes and dreams. In ancient mythology Neptune (known as Poseidon in Greek) was the god of the sea. The symbol for the planet Neptune in astrology is similar to the trident Neptune carried. Navigation in ancient times was precarious, and the changeable nature of Neptune held the fate of sailors in his hands. Would they reach dry land or be cast adrift into the depths? Such uncertainty could also be applied to Pisces. There is something elusive and a bit absentminded about Pisces that can be very endearing, yet some may feel they don't quite understand her. If Pisces is in touch with her soul's purpose and evolvement, she understands compassion more than any other sign does. If Pisces is adrift, however, then she tends to languish in her sensitivities and desires. These tendencies are also symbolized by the two Fish: one reaching upward toward the outside world, and the other downward, toward dreams and the inner self.

As a mutable sign, Pisces is flexible and goes with the flow. Instead of making a decision, Pisces may say "whatever." Decisions will creep up on her before she realizes what she is going to do. This passive approach has some drawbacks for her self-care: it may be too easy for her to float along, rather than guide the ship. Typically, Pisces also has trouble with time schedules. She rarely wears a watch and has to be in the rhythm of something before she can get to appointments on time.

Self-Care and Pisces

The first action in self-care for Pisces is to create comfort, order, color, and cleanliness in her home. Pisces is a natural at organization; this may be her way of creating a world on dry land that feels secure and controllable. Pisces can easily become overwhelmed by oceans of feelings, so knowing exactly where everything is soothes her.

A facet of the Pisces character that may be counterproductive to good self-care is that she can be easily swayed by the opinions of others. Unless she was raised with good nutrition and health habits, she takes a while to understand that taking care of herself requires effort and planning. She is particularly lax about eating regularly and though she is a water sign (and many water signs tend to prefer salty over sugary flavors), she can develop quite a sweet tooth. Additionally, Neptune, Pisces's ruler, also rules all drugs and alcohol. Any of the signs can have a tendency toward overindulgence, but Pisces's sensitivity and desire to retreat from the world can lead her to seek solutions or comfort in alcohol or other vices.

A far better way for Pisces to handle life's stresses is through a commitment to natural and alternative health practices. The first step is to straighten out her diet and fill in any holes in her vitamin or nutrient needs with supplements. Self-care regarding diet is necessary for everyone, but due to Pisces's especially sensitive system, she needs to take special care in good nutritional habits.

Another essential self-care practice for Pisces is to set aside "space out" time. This can be with music, meditation, or a walk in the country, or by coloring abstract designs in a coloring book. Pisces needs a controllable place to go for relaxation. While some signs flourish when spending a lot of their time socializing, Pisces quickly runs out of steam. To recoup her energies, she needs to be alone and in an unchallenging environment.

Pisces usually enjoys exercise as long as the surroundings are pleasant. She does well in sports because she has a natural sense of rhythm. Water sports are a great activity for her. She also enjoys horseback riding and aerobic dance, which also involve rhythm. In fact some of the greatest ballet dancers throughout history have been Pisces. Tai chi and gentle martial arts also appeal to her. Exercise such as this is where Pisces can effortlessly go with the flow.

Psychological self-care is also crucial for Pisces. Learning to articulate her feelings, such as through visits with a therapist, helps her move those feelings from silent worry to a definitive problem she can then solve. A sympathetic therapist who is in tune with Pisces's sensitivity will ensure counseling has a good effect.

Pisces Rules the Feet

Pisces rules over the feet. As the sign most connected to spirituality, Pisces needs her feet to be healthy in order to stay grounded on the earth. Comfortable shoes are a number one self-care item. For a Pisces woman, high heels are the enemy; eventually her feet will suffer long-term effects. Choose comfort over glamour, and consider orthotics if your feet are especially prone to soreness.

A weekly foot rub is a very good self-care practice for Pisces. She should also consider trying reflexology. Targeting specific organs in the body through different pressure points on the feet, reflexology is a simple practice that can ease many aches, pains, and negative emotions. Pisces should also pamper her feet with regular pedicures. The goal here is for Pisces to feel as comfortable on the ground as she does in the imagination.

Pisces and Self-Care Success

A potential pitfall to Pisces's continuing self-care is her forgetfulness. Pisces just might forget what her program is, or become lost in a poem until hours have passed and she has missed dinner. A beeper clock or watch, or a special alarm on a smartphone, is a great solution. Pisces can also get a lot of use out of a smart watch that can be programmed to send out reminders. Besides keeping Pisces on schedule, a smart watch can keep track of how much of her time was spent doing certain things that day. This will help orient Pisces and give her an idea of how her daily schedule is working out.

A second pitfall to good self-care is dependence on drugs or alcohol. Ruled by Neptune, Pisces is prone to indulgence that can turn into dependence. She should be very mindful of how much she drinks, et cetera. By keeping track of this, she will be able to understand how often she turns to these substances and why. Working with a doctor can also be helpful if Pisces feels she is unable to determine whether she is using drugs or alcohol responsibly. The tendency to overuse drugs or alcohol is not due to a weakness in Pisces's character. In fact it is the strength of her sensitivities in a world that does not always value feelings that can push Pisces toward these substances. By using her own sensitive feeling mechanism, Pisces can discover better ways to manage and express her individuality.

Lastly, for Pisces who are actively involved in caretaking professions such as nursing, social work, or counseling, it is easy to become overinvolved with other people's problems. Not only is Pisces an effective caregiver, but she also absorbs the energies of the person she is working with, which depletes her own energies over time. Learning to release the lingering thoughts and feelings after work ensures that Pisces practices the self-care that she preaches to others.

Pisces offers the final gift of the zodiac with her compassion and service to others. When Pisces learns that serving herself can magnify her ability to both help others and feel good all around, she provides a perfect model of self-care for friends and family. So let's take a look at some restorative self-care activities designed especially for you, Pisces.

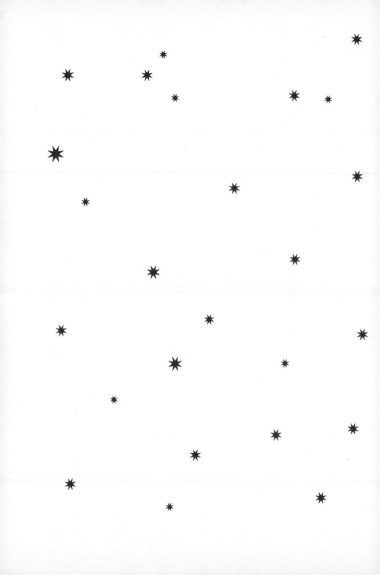

PART 2

SELF-CARE
RITUALS
— FOR —
PISCES

Treat Your Feet

Pisces rules the feet, so it is especially important for her to practice personal wellness routines that include foot care. Healthy, happy feet will keep Pisces well grounded. A frequent pedicure is a must; you can invest in trips to a spa, or get your own foot spa for easy home use.

Give your feet plenty of time to soak in the warm water and expel dirt and oils. Then use a pumice stone and natural lotions to remove dead skin cells and hydrate your skin. If you wish, go one step further and apply an aqua blue nail polish. This shade will look elegant, while also displaying your special connection to the ocean.

Get Motivated

If you find that you are feeling unmotivated to work out, start by listening to your favorite music to get amped up. Sometimes just feeling the beat can jump-start your energy level and get your blood flowing. If you are working out at home, you may even want to try dancing around as your entire workout. Dancing for 30 minutes is great cardio. Just blast your favorite tunes and let your body move naturally. Mix up the playlist tempo to keep things interesting. No slow songs allowed!

Savor Seafood Chowder

Pisces is quite the daydreamer. Constantly moving between creative ideas and deep emotions, she easily becomes lost in her own inner world. While this sets the stage for many of the things that make her so special, Pisces should also practice living in the moment. Root yourself in the present once in a while with a delicious experience.

If you like fish, a warm seafood chowder is the perfect meal for you, Pisces. Hearty and bursting with different flavors, this chowder is a tasty blend of comfort food and Pisces's astrological home, the ocean. Focus completely on the different ingredients of the meal as you eat, feeling the dish ease both mind and body into a peaceful, centered state. Savoring your food will also benefit your digestive system, which can get upset by fast eating. A healthy gut is a happy you.

Choose Flowing Exercises

As a water sign, you are drawn to fluid movements. When it comes to exercise, look for things that give your body freedom to move in the way it wants to. The last thing you want is to be restrained. Try tai chi or an aerobic dance class. Even Pilates can be soothing for water signs, as it helps build muscle and keeps you moving in a natural way.

Open Your Third Eye
with Aquamarine

P isces has a unique insight into the metaphysical realm; in fact, many people call her psychic. The perfect crystal for her to have on hand is aquamarine. This eye-catching blue stone promotes a higher level of consciousness by opening your third eye chakra.

Located on the forehead, the third eye chakra is an energy source that connects you to insight and subconscious knowledge. By opening this chakra, you can tap into a higher awareness of what drives you, your loved ones, and your community. Keeping an aquamarine crystal with you will help you turn creative ideas into actionable plans for the future.

Aquamarine can also be used to balance your emotions. As you release negative feelings, the powers of aquamarine will draw a sense of happiness and optimism to you. You can keep aquamarine in your pocket, display it in a central part of your home, or even wear it on a necklace or other piece of jewelry so it is always on hand.

Stick to a Routine

Routine can be boring for a water sign, but it is key to a solid self-care regimen. It may take discipline to stick to a routine, but without a well-constructed plan, apathy will take over and you'll find yourself doing nothing to improve your overall wellness. Make sure you vary your activities to keep things fresh and new. It may help to buy a large desk calendar and mark off when you are doing what activity. This will help keep you on track and will take any indecisiveness off the table.

Read Poetry

Poetry is one of the simplest yet deepest forms of self-expression. As an emotional and creative sign, Pisces will delight in exploring the passionate words of a poem. In fact she may even be inspired to write some poetry of her own!

Try reading poems by a kindred Pisces spirit. Ruled by misty Neptune, Pisces is a puzzle that few fully understand. So who better to tap into your unique experience than a fellow Pisces? Famous Pisces poets include W.H. Auden, Elizabeth Barrett Browning, and Dr. Seuss.

Make Water a Part of Your Life

You may think that all water signs are naturally drawn to water in every capacity, but this isn't necessarily true. Every water sign is different and has different preferences. While most water signs take comfort in water-based activities, such as swimming, diving, and water aerobics, others prefer to simply be near water, but not in it. Wherever you fall on this spectrum, water is an important grounding mechanism for you. It calms you, makes you feel safe, and helps orient you when you are feeling lost. Make water a part of your life in whatever way you feel most comfortable.

Put Those Feet Up!

Because Pisces rules the feet, a footstool would be a great addition to your décor or gift for a fellow Pisces. Pisces is often susceptible to problems with her feet, so having a soft spot where she can put them up, take some of the pressure off, and relax is right in line with her needs. For perfect Pisces style, look for fabrics in oceanic blues and greens, and the cozier and plusher the fabric, the better. Pisces loves the cozy factor!

Cuddle Up in Chenille

Pisces is known for being sensitive, and so is drawn to soft textures that soothe her soul and comfy surroundings that make her feel safe. Because of this desire to feel comfortable and cozy, Pisces tends to decorate her home in fabrics that elicit that feeling. Chenille fits this bill perfectly for Pisces. The feathery fabric is soft and silky with an almost velvety touch, perfect for wrapping around yourself and cuddling in. Invest in some chenille blankets for your home and your Pisces nature will thank you!

Stretch

The type of exercise you do as a water sign is very important. Many water signs have smooth muscles that do not usually bulk up, so doing exercises that are designed to add heft to your muscle won't be particularly beneficial. Instead, you should look for exercises that stretch your muscles, such as yoga. You don't even have to go to a yoga class to try it out. There are plenty of online videos for beginner yogis to try—just stick to the basics.

If yoga isn't your favorite, you can still make stretching an essential part of your wellness routine by stretching before and after every workout. It may even help to do some gentle stretches before bed to keep your muscles limber and flexible.

Play with Bubbles

Pisces is playful, without a doubt. She loves fantasizing about imaginary realms and sees the world with the same delight as a child. So why not indulge your childlike side and play with some bubbles? Buy a bubble gun and amuse yourself and any nearby kids with a flood of beautiful bubbles. Enjoy the soapy watery texture, watch the calming peaceful orbs float up to the sky, and create fantastical stories of where they might be going and who they might meet. Immerse yourself in the pure, simple joy of bubbles.

Watch Your Salt (and Water)

You've probably heard that our bodies are made up of more than 50 percent water. Water signs tend to hold on to water more than other signs do, which means they often have a softness to their faces and bodies. It may seem counterproductive, but drinking the right amount of water daily may, in certain circumstances, help reduce water retention, as well as flush toxins. Sometimes our bodies retain water in response to dehydration. Try to meet the recommended guidelines for how much water you should drink every day (depending on sex, lifestyle, climate, and health).

You can also watch how much salt you consume. Too much sodium (either in table salt or processed foods and soft drinks) increases your risk of water retention. If you do experience water retention symptoms, visit your doctor for advice.

Enjoy a Cup of Cocoa

Sometimes Pisces just needs to have a little alone time. What better way to spend a chilly evening than under your favorite blanket with a nice cup of hot chocolate? Add a spoonful of hazelnut spread, some vanilla extract, or top your mug off with some mini-marshmallows; you can personalize your mini-hibernation treat however you like! It's really about enjoying some relaxing time inside when it's too cold to be outside. This chilly night in will be the perfect chance to unwind. Put on your favorite playlist and just sit back and sip that chocolaty goodness.

Watch Your Favorite Tearjerker

It's okay to be emotional, Pisces. Every now and then, you just need a good, cathartic cry. You can achieve such a release in a private setting by setting up your very own movie night or Sunday afternoon matinee. This gives you the chance to relax on your couch and have a good cry—with plenty of Kleenex and snacks within reach. Whether your melancholy mood has you queueing up a classic or a recent release, it's time to turn off the lights and turn on the waterworks. Allowing yourself the opportunity to express your emotions is important for your overall well-being. Being able to do it while enjoying your favorite movie stars act is a win-win for everyone.

Turn to Nature

Stress happens to everyone; it's how you handle it that makes a difference. For water signs the best way to beat stress is to retreat to a safe space: nature. If you have the opportunity to spend time by a body of water, like a creek, river, or, ideally, the beach, do so as often as possible. Just listen to the sound the water makes as it moves, lapping against rocks or sand, and let the stress melt away from your muscles. If you don't have easy access to a body of water, download and listen to some water sounds outside. It's not quite the same, but it will mimic the calming experience of being by the water.

Collect Sea Glass

_____

Sea glass at a literal level is just pieces of glass that have been washed back onto the shore, but symbolically it is so much more than that. Sea glass begins as something discarded and broken, deemed useless. But then it is weathered, its sharp edges are worn away and smoothed out, and it is reborn again on the shore as something different. This rebirth from the sea resonates deeply with Pisces and her affinity to the water. It also sparks her empathetic personality and reminds her of how interactions with others can shape her in ways that she may never have thought possible.

Collect some sea glass next time you are by the shore, and display it in a clear glass bowl in your home. Place it somewhere the light can shine through it and illuminate the myriad colors, a reminder of how you, too, can weather a storm and emerge as something beautiful.

Laugh As Much As Possible

———————

Laughter can soothe the soul, especially the soul of a weary water sign. You tend to feel deeply, and need a healthy release to let go of those heavy emotions. Laughter can be that release. If you don't laugh, you may start to get bogged down with too many negative feelings. The only way to survive in life is to see the comedy in things. Water signs are especially good at this, but, sometimes, they need a little push. When you are feeling down, go to a funny movie or seek out a stand-up comedian putting on a show.

Decorate with Mermaids

Pisces likes to have her love of the sea reflected in her home décor. It wouldn't be uncommon to see images of seashells, starfish, corals, the ocean, or other aquatic themes in her home. So, when decorating your bathroom, bring a bit of the sea into the room with some mermaids. Mermaids are particularly good for decorating a bathroom where you get ready in the morning, because they represent independence, confidence, and the power to look deeper into a situation. These powerful sea guardians represent not only the beauty of the ocean but also its fierce strength, a fitting motivation for Pisces as she gets ready to tackle her day.

Avoid Crowds

Y ou are a sensitive soul, water sign, one who tends to absorb the vibrations and energy coming from other people. Because of this, it's best for you to avoid large crowds, especially if you are feeling vulnerable or sad. Being in a large group of strangers will just exacerbate those negative feelings you are struggling with, and may even make you feel more alone than you already do. Instead, stay home and allow yourself some quality relaxation time. Give yourself permission to lounge around and be lazy. Enjoy your own company!

Illuminate Your Home
with Stained Glass

Pisces loves stained-glass windows, and this is fitting considering this sign rules faith and churches. Bring this element of your sign into your home by buying a panel of stained glass. A form of stained glass that can hang in a window—or some other place that can catch the natural light and filter it into your home—would be the best, as opposed to a stained-glass lamp or other ornamentation. When the sun hits the glass, beams of color will burst into your home, filling it with a magical glow. Look for glass panels with aquatic themes to bring your water nature into your décor.

Wash It Off

As a water sign, you are used to being affected by other people's energy and the energy of the atmosphere around you. It is essential for your emotional health that you wash away any feelings you may have absorbed from others throughout the day. Make a point to take a shower or bath every night to cleanse your emotional aura. You may even find dry brushing before you bathe to be beneficial. Not only does dry brushing help loosen and remove dead skin from your body, it can be a wonderfully cathartic experience for water signs, especially if you envision the ritual as also sloughing away any emotional burdens you have picked up over the past few hours.

Embrace Your Duality
in Your Décor

One of the symbols of Pisces depicts the two Fish tied together but swimming in opposite directions, signifying the duality of this sign. Pisces is very adaptive and can make herself at home in almost any situation and with any group of people. She can often be a mediator between two different sides, and her dual nature allows her to see both sides of a situation. Embrace this dual nature of your sign by decorating with things that represent both your affinity to the sea and your life on land. Try images of mermaids on land, the shore where the ocean meets the sand, or waterfalls cascading down mountainsides.

Set Good Bathroom Vibes

Make your bathroom into the oasis you deserve! Having the perfect vessel to indulge your watery tendencies is essential for a water sign's self-care. Invest in a deep tub for your bathroom that you can soak in when you are feeling stressed—the deeper and roomier the better. Buy luxurious bubble baths and bath bombs to use when you draw a bath. Additionally, make sure that you have good water pressure for your shower. Lastly, choose bathroom tile that reflects water themes and colors, such as light blue, white, and green.

Enjoy a Bit of Chocolate

L ike the sea, there are many layers to complicated Pisces. She loves to look beneath the surface and discover that not everything is as it seems. That's why when looking for the perfect chocolate confection for your sign, you should try a liqueur-filled chocolate. Though many water signs may prefer less sweet flavors, Pisces can often get a hankering for sugary treats (just another layer to her complicated personality). Sweet on the outside with a little kick within, liqueur-filled chocolates perfectly suit your Pisces nature. Plus they are delicious and indulgent, and what Pisces wouldn't love that?

Keep It Simple

When it comes to fashion, water signs like to keep things simple and classic. Their favorite colors for clothing are muted tones, like navy blue, black, gray, and white, along with pops of color, like turquoise. Once a water sign finds a style that they are comfortable with, they'll stick to it. Changing their style requires a lot of energy, so it's easier for them to stay with what works.

Don't be surprised if it takes you a little while to get acclimated to a new fashion accessory or style of dressing. If you get the urge, though, do try out something new. You can always go back to your favorite staple items if you are uncomfortable.

Add a Scarf

Pisces is known for her flowy, soft, and comfortable style. She is not up for the ordinary in terms of fashion and is usually on the lookout for unique and artsy accessories that are still on the simple, sophisticated side. A fabulous scarf would be an ideal piece for Pisces as it perfectly suits her romantic and dreamy taste. In spring go for a bright scarf draped casually around your neck, and in the wintertime go for a comfy cowl scarf, which also appeals to Pisces's love of warmth and coziness.

Do Nighttime Activities

Some water signs are morning people, but most thrive in the nighttime hours. That's because the night calls to water signs. It is dark and peaceful, and they often feel that they are protected when the sun is down. If you are feeling vulnerable, plan a nighttime activity, such as stargazing, watching fireworks, or going for a simple drive or walk around your neighborhood with a friend. The key is to take some time to appreciate the quiet and calm that come with the evening hours, allowing the shift from chaotic day to tranquil night to ease your mind.

Try Some Poppy Seeds

Not only does the poppy flower symbolize imagination, a concept near and dear to Pisces, but the seeds of the flower may have tremendous health benefits for Pisces (providing she is not allergic to poppy seeds). Poppy seeds contain a unique combination of calcium and manganese that may prove beneficial for muscle function and bone health.

In addition, poppy seeds may help improve mental health by regulating neurotransmitters that can improve cognition. So get more poppy seeds into your diet. Try them on bagels, in muffins, in salad dressings, or added to dishes such as chicken salad or oatmeal. Be aware, though, that consumption of poppy seeds before a toxicology screening can result in a false positive test.

Sail Off to Sleep

Fortunately, water signs tend to fall asleep relatively easily, but they can sometimes become distracted if their environment isn't conducive to sleep. At night it's beneficial to use room-darkening curtains to keep any light from creeping in. Water signs like to sleep in complete darkness, and may even find it difficult to sleep if their room isn't pitch black. Using blackout shades and dark heavy curtains will help make your bedroom cozy and dark, just the way water signs like it. Alternatively, you may consider using a sleeping mask to prevent any light from bothering you while you sleep.

Get Cozy

There's nothing quite like taking a long bath or shower and then snuggling up in a thick bath towel. For water signs self-care means pampering yourself with luxury whenever you can. A simple way to do this is to invest in high-quality towels or a robe that you can wear after you've washed away any negative emotions from the day. The soft, fluffy material will help you feel safe and protected. If you have the opportunity, consider buying a towel warmer as well.

Try a Taste of Caviar

Pisces loves the wildly romantic and often indulges her cravings. Champagne and caviar? Yes, please! But caviar is more than just a decadent treat for Pisces. It also resonates with her love of all things related to the salty sea, and is a food that can help her mental state as well. Pisces, because of her empathy and compassion, is often susceptible to depression. Historically, caviar was once prescribed to alleviate depression. In fact recent studies show that caviar has high doses of omega-3 fatty acids, which may improve mood. So find your happy, quite literally, with caviar.

Go It Alone

When it comes to sports and leisure, water signs tend to do best with activities that take place outside and don't involve a lot of people. This means that team sports aren't always the best option for you. Water signs should avoid recreational leagues that attract a lot of people. Instead, they do better with low-pressure activities that focus on nature, such as walking, hiking, and climbing. You may find that you, as a water sign, don't really like competition, and there's absolutely nothing wrong with that.

Find an activity out in nature that suits you best. If you feel like you want some company, invite a few trusted friends along to join you.

Feel the Luxurious Softness
of Velvet

Pisces loves the feeling of coziness, and in wintertime would rather stay in her cavern of soft warm blankets than venture out into the cold air. But as she can't remain a hermit all winter long (although wouldn't that be nice!), Pisces should indulge in a velvet jacket when she does venture out into the brisk weather. The plush and luxe fabric of velvet matches perfectly with Pisces's love of opulence, and its softness and warmth resonate with her love of the cozy and comforting. So, if you must go out into the cold of winter, wrap yourself in velvet and feel the luxury of this distinctively soft fabric.

Get Cooking

Cooking and baking are wonderful outlets for water signs, though when given the choice, they tend to stick to the basics they've already mastered rather than experiment with new recipes. After all, if you have a handful of staple dishes that you know you can create easily and well, why would you want to try something new and risk it tasting terrible? Comfort food in particular appeals to a hungry water sign. Everything from macaroni and cheese to mashed potatoes and pancakes are usually big hits. So, why not keep your experimentation to your preferences, and buy a comfort food cookbook that can help expand your repertoire of recipes?

Take a Beach Vacation

Indulge the innate connection you have to water by taking a vacation to an island or near a beach. Being by the water will help recharge your batteries when you are feeling depleted. The warm weather in most tropical locations is perfect for a water sign who is hoping to lounge by the beach or pool and let their worries fade away.

Look for vacation destinations that also include water activities, such as lessons in paddle boarding or snorkeling, to help you connect with your element. If you can swing an all-inclusive resort, you'll get even more bang for your buck, with food, lodging, entertainment, and drinks included.

Spice Up a Meal with Star Anise

Many Pisces enjoy the flavor of star anise. Though many water signs tend to avoid spicier foods, Pisces can take a bit of heat, and a small amount of a spice like star anise is just the thing to inspire her creativity without knocking her watery nature out of balance.

Not to be confused with anise seed (and not Japanese star anise, which is actually poisonous), Chinese star anise is often used in Asian cooking and provides a warm, licorice flavor to dishes. Star anise appeals to Pisces's love of the exotic, and it is also filled with antioxidants and antibacterial properties that benefit her health as well. Include some in your favorite muffins or soup recipe.

Find Some Privacy

You may have noticed that, as a water sign, you need quiet and privacy to get your work done. When it comes to your job, you will be more productive working in a cubicle or by yourself than in an open-plan office or large group. You tend to get overwhelmed when you have too many people around you, so when you really need to concentrate, try retreating to your own secluded space. This will help keep you away from all the hustle and bustle, and limit your distractions.

When you feel the need to talk to others, a communal kitchen or break room is your ideal space. This is where you can comfortably mingle with coworkers before going back to your cubbyhole to get some work done. If you have a job where a group environment is highly valued, try speaking to your supervisor and letting them know how you work best. You might be surprised by how understanding they will be!

Get Out on a Boat

It's no surprise that Pisces loves the water and that the ideal spot for her to unwind would be on a boat. Got a special occasion coming up that you want to celebrate with family and friends? Hire a yacht for a night of luxury and fun on the seas. Yacht not in your budget? How about renting a canoe from a livery for a trip with friends? No matter how you do it, getting out on the water in a boat is an ideal activity for this water sign and one that will make you feel relaxed and in your zone.

Seek Out a Sauna or Steam Room

The benefits of a sauna or steam room go far beyond simple stress relief. Sitting in a sauna or steam room can improve your circulation, ease muscle pain, and help with some skin problems. For water signs, taking a sauna is a great way to cleanse the soul and calm the mind. Look to see if a local gym or spa has one you can use. Sit and let the dry heat of the sauna or the hot steam of the steam room surround you and loosen the stress in your body.

If you don't have access to a stream room, you can create your own budget version by turning your shower on hot for a few minutes, shutting the door and windows, and letting the room fill with steam. Sit in a towel and enjoy the sensation of moisture floating all around you!

Take Ice-Skating Lessons

E ven frozen water has a special place in a water sign's heart. Just because you can't see the water moving and hear it lapping doesn't mean it is any less soothing or refreshing! In fact, ice can be invigorating for a water sign. Try embracing your cold side by taking beginners' ice-skating lessons. A number of world-class ice-skaters have been water signs. If you already have had some practice and aren't in the mood for a full lesson, try going to a local skating rink and just skate on your own for a little while. You may find that the smooth cut of the blade over ice soothes you.

Take a Houseboat Vacation

C ontact with the water is essential for Pisces. Not only does she find it peaceful and relaxing, but it helps ground her and gives her an inner feeling of contentment. So next time you are planning a vacation, why not consider renting a houseboat? From a houseboat you can better enjoy the serenity of the water you are on, and you get to experience the lake, river, or sea firsthand. In addition the rocking sensation of the water under the boat is soothing for Pisces, and can be just what she needs if she is having sleeping problems.

A houseboat also perfectly suits Pisces's escapist personality. If she gets bored of her current location or the people in it, she can start the engine and venture off to another destination.

Unleash Your Inner Ballet Dancer

Neptune, Pisces's ruling planet, is also the planet that governs dance, so it's only natural that Pisces would love ballet. Not only does Pisces love going to watch the ballet, but she has a natural talent for it as well. A workout with fluid motion is ideal for Pisces, and one that enables her to show and release emotion is right up her alley. Look into your local health club or even online videos for ballet-focused workouts. You will get a great dose of exercise, but you'll also feel the cathartic release of expressing your feelings through motion.

Find Luck with Seahorses

The seahorse is a sacred symbol to Neptune in Roman mythology, and with just cause. The seahorse has long been considered a symbol of good luck, and stories from ancient times told of how seahorses would safely guide drowned sailors to their places in the afterlife. In fact sailors would often use images of seahorses as good luck charms. Known as a calm and patient creature, the seahorse reminds you to enjoy who you are and be patient with yourself. Try adding seahorse motifs to your home for beauty and luck, and if you ever find an actual seahorse, that is especially lucky!

Learn Something New

Mentally, water signs can understand a whole concept quickly because they intuitively feel it, rather than logically piece it together. The details are not important to them; all they need is to trust their gut and the emotions they are feeling inside. Their empathy is what helps them understand.

Use this superpower by learning something new—topics like philosophy and religion are a great place for water signs to start. These categories often require your ability to grasp a larger concept and understand things at a holistic level, rather than memorize detailed facts and figures. You may even find it beneficial to watch documentaries or listen to lectures in addition to reading a book—whatever sparks your passion!

Buy Fashion for Your Legs

Pisces rules the feet, so it is no surprise that fashion for the feet and legs is a delight for her. Not only are comfortable shoes in an array of colors and styles a must for Pisces, but so are colorful socks, tights, leggings, and other kinds of stockings. The more unique and whimsical the better, as Pisces loves fun and flirty accents that give her classic wardrobe a touch of excitement without going over the top. Try finding clothing in your signature colors of sea-green, blues, and other pastels to make the look truly Pisces-worthy.

Try a Boxing Workout

While water signs don't usually respond well to exercises that require a lot of repetition, a boxing workout is definitely an exception. In fact, a few world champion boxers over the years have been water signs. Boxing workouts are a great emotional and physical release if you've been feeling stressed or angry. The power and strength you'll feel when you learn with an expert to kick, punch, and duck properly will keep you coming back to the gym for more. Initially, you may find it difficult to get used to the new motions, but once your body adapts, boxing training is actually a very fluid activity, perfect for water signs! Look into beginners' classes in your local area.

Pick Up a Good Book

As an emotional and reflective sign, Pisces needs plenty of time alone to relax and recharge her batteries. One of the best ways to unwind is by reading a book. Pisces will delight in getting lost in a great story, setting her many thoughts aside for a few hours and refocusing them on an intriguing plot. But what books will Pisces enjoy?

Pisces is a romantic and nurturing sign, so she loves tales of love—from passionate affairs to the bond between a parent and child. With her special gift of insight, she is also unafraid to explore themes that will make her think. The masterful works of Pisces authors such as Victor Hugo and Amy Tan may top her list.

Indulge in Rainy Days

Some water signs prefer moody, cool, gray weather to bright sunshine. If you have the opportunity, indulge in a rainy day by staying inside, snuggling up on the couch, and listening to the rain beating down outside. You may choose to read a book or listen to music, whatever feels right. If you are feeling adventurous, you may even want to go for a walk in the rain. Make sure you have the right equipment—every water sign should have a decent raincoat and pair of rain boots. Check the weather forecast often to stay ahead of any potential rainy days.

Express Your Feelings

You feel so deeply, water sign, it's only natural that sometimes your emotions spill over and become overwhelming. Water signs are often receptive and inwardly focused. While you are very good at recognizing your feelings, you find it difficult to express them to others. You have trouble articulating what's inside. Instead, you would prefer that your loved ones just understand what you are feeling rather than having to explain it to them.

Practice expressing your emotions by keeping a journal. At least once a day, preferably at night after you've spent the day processing emotions, write down how you feel. If you are struggling with where to begin, start with the words *I feel* and go from there. Remember that no one will ever read this journal unless you want them to, so don't feel self-conscious. Just write what feels natural.

Keep Photo Memories

Scrapbooks, photo albums, and iPhone picture galleries are all treasures to water signs. They love to flip through their favorite memories and reminisce about old times or relive their happiest moments.

Spend time putting together collections of photos that chronicle each part of your life. You can organize them in whatever way feels right to you. The goal is to make sure you are surrounded by your most cherished memories at all times. You may even consider putting together a photo collage that you can frame and hang on the wall. You can indulge your love of photos even further by creating a scrapbook or online photo book for your loved ones on their birthdays. The personal touch will bring tears and smiles.

Ground Yourself with Bach's Clematis

D reamy Pisces always has her head in the clouds. While this is great for sparking new ideas and creating moving works of art, sometimes a little extra focus is in order. Clematis essence is the perfect nature aid for gently bringing you back to reality so you can concentrate on the here and now.

The essence of this simple white flower can be found diluted in the original Bach Flower Remedies. Try adding a couple of drops of Bach's clematis remedy to a glass of water (follow the directions on the bottle) and drinking slowly. (The Bach Flower Remedies are available online.)

Embrace Your Sentimental Side

Whether they are celebrating birthdays, Christmas, or Valentine's Day, water signs love the holidays and any happy occasion. You especially love the sentimentality of tradition. Think about all the ways you can participate in holiday or birthday customs with the people you love. This may mean cooking a special meal for everyone, setting up decorations, or just spending time catching up with family and friends. Use your creative side to start new traditions, and encourage your loved ones to get involved. These rituals will help you feel closer to the people you cherish most.

Try Hypnotherapy

————————

Pisces is connected to the subconscious. A great way to tap further into your subconscious is through hypnotherapy. Hypnotherapy facilitates access to this part of the brain by quieting your consciousness so that those deeper thoughts and feelings can be heard. A trained hypnotherapist will use calming techniques to move you into a completely relaxed state, where you can dive into your subconscious. By discovering your deepest drives and fears, you can then move toward managing them in ways that aid your overall growth.

In fact hypnotherapy may help relieve many ailments, from anxiety and insomnia, to chronic pain and addictive habits. If you are considering hypnotherapy, ask your doctor for local recommendations.

Make Water a Part of
Your Sleep Routine

While many water signs don't have trouble falling asleep, you may find that turning on a sound machine that features the sounds of rain, waves, or running water will make you feel more relaxed when you are drifting off to dreamland. Some water signs find that they are distracted by their emotions when they are trying to go to sleep. They replay things that happened throughout the day and relive how those things made them feel instead of quieting their minds. Sound machines can help focus your mind and ward off any distractions. Simply breathe deeply and listen to the sounds around you, and you'll be asleep in no time.

Strike a Fish Pose

The Fish Pose is the perfect yoga position for Pisces, as it connects her to her astrological symbol, the Fish, and also increases flexibility while opening up the heart chakra. The heart chakra is responsible for emotions and your connection to others. As a compassionate sign, Pisces benefits from balancing her feelings and being mindful of the give and take within her relationships.

To do this pose, lie on your back with your knees bent and feet on the floor. Lift your pelvis slightly off the floor, sliding your hands, palms down, under your rear. On an inhale, with slightly bent elbows, press your forearms and elbows firmly against the floor and begin to lift your chest, creating an arch in the upper back. Draw your shoulder blades into your back and lift your upper torso and head away from the floor. Tilt your head back, resting it lightly on the yoga mat. Pause for three breaths. Inhale and slightly raise your head off the floor. Then gently lower your torso and head back onto the floor as you exhale.

Stay Grounded

———————————

It is important for water signs to live close to water (or visit it as often as possible) as a way of staying grounded. A view of some body of water from your home window will orient you and keep you stable, especially when you are feeling vulnerable or over-whelmed by your emotions. Seeing water can bring balance to your life that you would otherwise miss. The closer you can get to the water, the better. Watch out for high-rise apartments, though, even if they have a great view of water in the distance. Being up high can make water signs feel lost and aimless, as if they have no roots.

Keep It Candid

Pisces puts her feet to good work, always being on the move. While you don't want life to pass you by, you should also take a moment to capture it. A great way to stay true to your artistic spirit while on the go is by taking quick candid photos throughout the day. Don't bother posing or waiting for the perfect setup—capture the moment in the moment. You could even start a social media account dedicated to these photos. While it may seem a little silly, it's giving you the opportunity to see everything you do from a different perspective. These quick snapshots of your daily life will be an artful mosaic for you to reflect back on.

Decorate with Ocean Hues

Your home is a reflection of who you are and what you love. Water signs need a calming and soothing environment to thrive in, and the first way to accomplish this is to surround yourself with colors that are reminiscent of water. Look for muted, cool tones like light blue, gray, and deep green, accented with splashes of vibrant, warm colors like red and orange. You may even want to try painting a mural or pattern that makes you think of water on one of your walls. Above all, your home should be comfortable and familiar to you. Use color to make it your own.

Share Your Signature Cocktail

———————

Pisces loves sharing both her time and favorite treats with her friends and family members. Slip off to an oceanside oasis, and bring your loved ones along with you, with the sea breeze cocktail. This tropical refreshment is a delicious companion to any cookout, beach gathering, or dinner party. It will quickly become watery Pisces's signature libation.

To mix up some sea breezes for you and your loved ones, simply add 8 ounces vodka, 15 ounces cranberry juice, and 6 ounces grapefruit juice to a cocktail shaker filled with ice. Shake well, and then pour into a chilled glass and garnish with a frozen lime wedge.

Buy an Aquarium

Just because you don't live right next to a body of water doesn't mean you can't make the aquatic a part of your everyday life. One of the easiest ways to bring the ocean home is to invest in an aquarium. As a water sign, you'll find solace in the cool blue ripples of the water and the fluid movement of the fish swimming by. It's true that keeping a healthy aquarium does require research, advice from experts, money, and time, but the cost is well worth the benefits you'll see almost instantly in your mood.

Make a To-Do List

As an emotional sign who makes it her personal mission to help everyone around her, Pisces can sometimes become overwhelmed by the weight of everyone else's problems, coupled with her own many feelings. A great way to release some of this stress, and gain back a feeling of control over your surroundings, is by tackling small tasks around your home or office. Little chores can pile up fast, and they weigh on you more than you may realize.

Make a to-do list of easy items and devote your time to crossing them off one by one. The act of completing things that you may have set aside in the past alleviates stress, leaving you with a great feeling of accomplishment.

Don't Go to the Desert

Dry climates don't suit water signs well. You need to feel moisture in the air in order to breathe easy. While it's not advisable for water signs to live in a dry climate like the desert, if you do, there are certain things you can try to keep the air around you moist. The easiest is to research and purchase a humidifier for your home and run it as needed. This will significantly improve the quality of the air.

You can also look for an essential oil diffuser that uses water, which not only adds moisture to the air, but also diffuses essential oils to impact your mood. Experiment with different scents to find the one that is right for you.

Create a Personal Altar

Often described as psychic, Pisces is a sign that lives beyond the borders of the material world. Tap into your higher conscious with a small personal altar. An altar can be used to connect you to your spirituality, ward off negative energy, and celebrate the metaphysical. Create your own altar in your home by decorating a shelf or small table with candles, healing crystals, and other objects that you feel deeply linked to. You can also burn sage when meditating at your altar, as it is a traditional herb in many spiritual practices.

Skip the Spicy Foods

Water signs can be picky when it comes to their diet and nutrition. For example, they usually don't like spicy food and tend to stick to more muted cuisines, with the exception of salami and cured meats. The salty taste of these treats appeals to them. In fact, you may find you have more cravings for salty foods than sweet foods. That's not to say you don't like something sweet every now and again. A small piece of candy or baked good is all you need. Water signs also love carbs and will never pass up a piece of pizza when offered, though they are partial to pizza with meat toppings instead of vegetable toppings. So listen to your body, skip the spicy, and choose the foods that most appeal to your taste buds *and* your nutritional needs. Bon appétit!

Find a Muse

As an artistic sign of the zodiac, Pisces often uses mediums such as painting, drawing, and poetry to express her many intense emotions. It's important that you have things that feed your inspiration. To avoid creative dry spells, seek out a muse that encourages your artistic side. To find your muse, consider what speaks to your creative soul. This can be a person, a place, or even an activity that sparks expression. What ignites your passion? Is there a place you have visited that made you feel inspired? Is there someone you look to for motivation?

Stay Away from Strong Scents

Have you ever noticed that you are very sensitive to scents and often get headaches or feel nauseated when you are around heavy perfumes or colognes? Water signs have a very keen sense of smell, which can be a superpower, but also a hindrance at times. To avoid being overloaded with an offending smell, it's best for you to avoid sharing elevators or enclosed spaces with anyone wearing a heavy scent. It will stick to your clothes and linger around you all day. You should especially stay away from the perfume section in any department stores!

Invest in Comfortable Shoes

Pisces rules the feet, so good shoes are an essential part of her wardrobe. The feet are where your being connects to the physical world. And as a sign who is often lost in daydreams, Pisces should try to be firmly grounded to reality to avoid forgetting her earthly commitments and responsibilities. Invest in comfortable footwear, and consider extra support such as shoe inserts if you find your feet are easily irritated. You can also learn dozens of foot massage techniques online to ease pain.

Cherish Family Heirlooms

———————————

Family is very important to you as a water sign. You take comfort in the familial connections you have, and take pride in your loyalty to family no matter what. Because of this, your bond to your family only grows stronger day by day.

Every family is unique and has their own collection of heirlooms that are passed down from generation to generation. Display your own family heirlooms proudly. They are a special link to your ancestors and show off who you truly are.

Magnetize Love with
a Special Potion

———————

Pisces is a sign of love in every form. From romance to friendship, she is a role model for passion and care. If you find yourself losing a bit of that loving feeling, whether it is in the wake of a bad experience or due to stress, draw affection to you with a potpourri love potion. A love potion uses both natural elements and your inner energy to evoke love, typically of a romantic nature.

You can make your own by mixing simmering fresh water with spices, such as cinnamon and clove, and dried petals from flowers that symbolize love, such as roses, lilacs, or lavender. As you mix the potion, focus on your goal, envisioning it becoming a reality. Your home will be filled with the fragrance of love, drawing affection back into your life!

Surround Yourself
with Succulents

Succulents are some of the easiest plants to care for—some can grow well in indoor environments and require less frequent watering. These are the perfect plants for a busy water sign. Jade is a particularly popular choice—it is known as the lucky tree, or the money tree, and needs very little care to thrive. The color of the flowers that bloom from the plant can be either pink or white. Not only are succulents beautiful to look at, but surrounding yourself with green is a great way to reduce stress and create a calming, nurturing environment. Succulents can also increase productivity and concentration, so consider placing one near your workstation as well.

Enjoy a Glass of Red Wine

Red wine is a Pisces favorite. As a romantic sign, Pisces appreciates the seductive scent and taste of a great glass of red wine. It is also a classic touch in an intimate dinner for two, pairing perfectly with a pair of glowing candlesticks and a delicious meal. Set the mood, or romance yourself a little, by sipping your favorite red wine.

Be sure to savor it through all five senses—maybe even pretend you are leading a sophisticated wine tasting (from the comfort of your own home). Delight in the satisfying pop of the wine cork, and then take in the different scents and appearance of the wine once it is poured into your glass. Next, slowly sample the flavors and note the feel of the wine as it warms your throat. For an extra-romantic twist, try a sparkling wine with fresh fruit garnishes.

Meditate Alone

Spiritual practices such as meditation are best done alone for water signs. That's because meditation is a time of emotional vulnerability, and water signs are highly sensitive to other people's energies. If you are meditating with a group, you may inadvertently absorb other people's feelings rather than focus on your own. Instead, find a comfortable, private area where you can let your guard down and feel safe. Make sure your meditation spot is relaxing and inviting, with a soft seat and soothing ambiance. It may help to listen to quiet music or put on a sound machine to keep you focused.

Keep Electronics
Out of the Bedroom

Falling asleep can sometimes be difficult for Pisces. As an emotional sign, she is often filled with many feelings and thoughts throughout the day, which are hard to quiet when it is time for bed. Keeping your electronics out of the bedroom at night will remove those tempting stimulants that keep your mind and body up past bedtime. Also, avoid using your phone for the last half hour to one hour before bed. Ensure you get that precious beauty sleep you need.

Chase Your Wanderlust

———————

Sticking close to home is a comfort for many water signs. It's okay to prefer staying in to going out, but you should try to challenge your homebody habit by booking a trip somewhere far away every now and again. You may initially feel anxious about being away from home, but the excitement of seeing far-off, different lands may outweigh the discomfort. The good news is, as long as the room you stay in while traveling is comfortable, you'll be able to feel safe. Water signs just need a secure place to rest their heads, and they'll be able to enjoy new places without too much worry.

Accent Your Spaces
with African Violets

A frican violets are the perfect natural accent for the Pisces home and work space. These beautiful purple flowers symbolize deep, everlasting love. As a romantic water sign, Pisces is fueled by the strong relationships she has with partners, friends, and family members alike. Just like Pisces, the African violet is also linked to water and feminine energy, including passion and creativity. Keeping an African violet plant in spaces where you work or create will inspire your special gift for artistic expression.

Adopt a Dog or Cat

The world is broken up into dog people and cat people. While there are many people who enjoy both types of domesticated animals, they usually have a preference for one over the other. Water signs are definitely more cat people, but have been known to fall in love with small dogs as well.

Cats are independent and curious, traits that water signs appreciate. Small dogs can be outgoing and rambunctious (depending on their breed), also characteristics that appeal to a sometimes moody water sign. The key for water signs is finding a small animal to share your space with, one that fits well into the home you've already created for yourself. Just make sure to get expert advice on adopting (and properly caring for) your chosen pet from a local animal shelter before you commit.

Listen to Lute Music

———————

L ute music is very soothing, and Pisces loves calming sounds. The soft, often playful notes of the lute can balance Pisces's many emotions. This instrument is also rooted in history as a source of entertainment for nobility, beginning in ancient Egypt—a touch of artistic sophistication that Pisces will enjoy. Bring lute music into your home, specifically to spaces where you relax and recharge. A playlist of lute music on a low volume provides the perfect backdrop for your home oasis, helping you feel fully at peace and ready to dive into your many creative hobbies.

Spend Time with Loved Ones

Even though water signs are homebodies, they do like to socialize when the environment is just right. This usually means hanging out with a small group of close family members or friends. Water signs need to be surrounded by people they trust to feel comfortable enough to kick back and relax.

If you aren't in the mood to venture out beyond your front door, consider inviting your friends or family over for a small dinner party where you can all enjoy one another's company and speak candidly about your thoughts and emotions. This is a water sign's dream get-together!

Visit a Reflexologist

As you know, Pisces rules the feet. What you might not know is how much your feet rule the rest of your body. According to reflexology, the different areas of your feet correspond to different areas of your body—from your nose and sinuses to your knees and intestines. If there is something that is ailing you or you feel unbalanced, book yourself an appointment with a reflexologist. The reflexologist will realign your chi, or life force, by working the pressure points on your feet. The eyes may be the windows to the soul, but your feet could be the key to soothing that sore throat, relieving your back pain, and more.

Take In a Concert

L ive music is invigorating for many water signs. While being in crowds can sometimes be over- whelming for them, the positive energy of the music can help them overcome that discomfort. There's nothing quite like singing along to one of your favorite songs live. Surrender to the spirit of the music and let it permeate your being.

If you have the opportunity, look for an outdoor concert where you can combine your love of nature with the power of live music. During the summer months you'll find outdoor music festivals popping up all over the world that attract a variety of artists and fans. Find one that speaks to your unique musical taste!

Wrap Up in Silk

S ilk offers a smooth, watery feel that can calm the mind and help you feel relaxed. As an emotional and compassionate sign, Pisces can often absorb the feelings of those around her, leaving her feeling overwhelmed or scrambling to solve everyone's problems. Wearing a silk robe is a simple way to ease stress through the powers of touch. This timeless addition to your lounging wardrobe will be your ticket to some luxurious alone time. Choose colors that promote peace and a happy mood, such as light blue or yellow.

Attend the Ballet or Opera

As a water sign, you are driven by emotion and feeling. This is why you may feel such an inherent draw toward the performing arts, like dance and theater. Indulge this love by attending a ballet or opera performance in your area. Ballet is a beautiful example of the fluidity of motion, which speaks to water signs on a visceral level, and opera presents a vivid story through the power of song and language. Attending the opera can be a very emotional experience for the audience, so bring your tissues, water sign!

Peer Into a Crystal Ball

Pisces is a sign of deep insight—not just into her own subconscious, but into the subconscious of the entire world around her. A crystal ball isn't just a fabulous addition to the Pisces home or work space. It also promotes strong Pisces insight, and delights her love for magic. Sometimes even psychic Pisces has difficulty seeing through the fog. Struggling with a decision? Unsure of the answer to a current dilemma? Simply peer into your crystal ball when your intuitive powers are in need of a little boost.

Create Your Own Water Feature

Running water is soothing to water signs at work and at home. Purchase a small water fountain that you can keep near your desk at work to help you through stressful moments. When you are feeling overwhelmed, take a few moments to focus on the sound of the water and nothing else. You can leave the fountain running all day to help keep you feeling balanced and calm. If you have space at home, purchase another water fountain for your living room, or wherever you spend the most time. The trickling water will keep you company whenever you need it.

Spending time outdoors is also beneficial for water signs, so look for a water fountain that can be set up on a deck or in your backyard.

Feel Connected with Ylang-Ylang

Pisces is a sign of reflection and daydreams—but it is just as important that she have an open flow of communication with people in the physical world. As a compassionate water sign, she feels balanced when her relationships are strong and well cared for. An ingredient found in many perfumes, ylang-ylang promotes social connections and a feeling of intimacy in your relationships. You can very sparingly dab the essential oil (diluted according to instructions; use with caution if you have sensitive skin) on your neck, or diffuse it in a communal space such as your living room. It also boosts overall mood and energy levels (which is helpful when there are things to do, but your bed is calling your name).

Embrace Your Love of History

Water signs love to travel to different times in their imaginations—that's why historical fiction is the perfect genre for this literary sign. Why not turn that love of different time periods into an excuse to actually visit those historical sites?

Make a list of sites that you have always wanted to see, and start visiting. Studying history requires that you imagine yourself in the same situations as the people of that time. As a water sign, you are incredibly empathetic and understanding, so this skill probably comes easily to you. Use it to your advantage and relive some of the most important moments in history with your own eyes.

Promote Calm with Lotus Flowers

The lotus flower is the perfect image for Pisces to include in her home or office. As a sign filled with emotions and ideas, Pisces can become overwhelmed by everything racing through her head. Simple yet eye-catching, the white Japanese lotus encourages calm, and can be useful in refocusing your mind and quieting all of the thoughts and feelings that you are experiencing. Frame a photograph of a lotus to place on your desk or hang in your home, or purchase other lotus accents to decorate spaces you frequent each day.

Trust Your Intuition

Do you sometimes find that you intuitively know what time it is without even checking your watch or phone? That's because water signs have a great internal sense of time. You're probably always early to your appointments, and don't even need to set an alarm to wake up in the morning.

Learn to trust your intuition more in all parts of your life, not just when it comes to being on time. As a water sign, you can usually trust your gut instinct. You have a talent for reading situations and people through how you feel. This is a strength that you can rely on. Don't second-guess yourself so much—learn to listen to that voice in your mind. It's usually right!

Sip Black Tea

B lack tea is the perfect daytime beverage for Pisces! Black tea contains caffeine, as well as an amino acid that can help you stay focused. Day-dreamer Pisces can sometimes use this extra boost of concentration to get things done. Black tea is also full of antioxidants and may promote a healthy gut, reduce blood pressure, and boost heart health!

Take a little time to mull things over as you sip the tea before that energy boost kicks in. You can find many different types of black teas, from Earl Grey to Darjeeling, so do a little experimenting to find your favorite.

Go to Therapy

_____

While water signs have a lot of emotions swirling around inside, classic therapy might not work for them. They don't like to get stuck living in the past, mulling over things that have already happened. To them, the past is a bottomless well of memory. When it comes to talking about their feelings, they prefer to focus on targeted problems. However, they can certainly benefit from the journey.

If you are considering therapy, ask your doctor for recommendations, and then look around for a therapist who understands exactly what you are looking to get out of your sessions. It may take some trial and error, but eventually you'll find the right professional and right approach for you.

Learn about Edgar Cayce

Ruled by misty Neptune, Pisces is a sign of special insight that some would call psychic. Reconnect with your metaphysical talents by reading about fellow Pisces, Edgar Cayce. Born in 1877, Cayce was a clairvoyant and became America's most well-known trance medium healer.

During his trances, Cayce would provide readings for people, including cures for numerous ailments, insight into an individual's past lives, and predictions of the future. Over 14,000 of his readings can be found on record at the Association for Research and Enlightenment in Virginia Beach, Virginia. His connection to the metaphysical will both resonate with and fascinate Pisces.

Depend on Your Water Friends

Sometimes, in order to really work through a problem, you need to turn to someone who just intuitively understands you. For water signs this means seeking out other water signs. They are usually just as good at listening as you are, and can help you work through whatever is going on in your life at the time. Since water signs are so sympathetic, they will always be around to lend an ear when you need it. It is important for water signs to support one another, especially when it comes to their emotional health and balance.

Spritz Rosewater

Romantic Pisces adores roses. From the vibrant color of the petals to the sweet scent, roses are the perfect symbol of Pisces's favorite thing: love. And the benefits of the rose extend far beyond a romantic gesture or pretty centerpiece. In fact many know rosewater to be an essential beauty potion that works wonders on your skin. A bit of the water dabbed on the skin helps tighten your pores and remove excess oils. Combined rosewater and glycerin products are also available to double the skin benefits.

Additionally, rosewater is also a great natural aid for balancing emotions. The scent boosts your mood and calms anxious thoughts. It also helps you feel relaxed, so consider spritzing your pillow before bed for a restful sleep. No matter your intended use, always have an atomizer of rosewater handy.

Chant Your Way to Calm

As a water sign, you may become easily over-whelmed by a lot of noise, but chanting may have the reverse effect on you if you are looking to relax and zen out. For centuries Buddhist monks have used chanting as a way to prepare the mind for meditation. You, too, can use this ritual to find peace. Repetitive chanting often mimics the ebb and flow of water, something that innately pleases water signs. Try researching a few chants that you can use in the comfort of your own home. When you are ready to meditate, start chanting, and repeat the words over and over again until a sense of calm sweeps over you.

Give Someone You Love
an Orchid

Orchids are Pisces-ruled. With their vibrant colors and exotic appearance, orchids have a long-standing association with love. Share them with a special someone! It will brighten both of your days. Compassionate Pisces places great importance in deep, strong bonds, so she will delight in this simple way of showing someone how much she cares.

The color of your orchid will also say a lot about your feelings. Go for yellow when gifting an orchid to a friend, pink for a romantic partner, orange for that office crush, and purple for someone you greatly admire.

Meditate with Crystals

_____

Employing the help of the right crystal at the right time can do wonders for balancing your energy and emotions. Look for crystals that are reminiscent of the ocean, such as blue lace agate, aquamarine, and lapis lazuli. Blue lace agate can calm anxiety and worry, aquamarine promotes courage and communication, and lapis lazuli can help you discover the truth about yourself and your life. When you are meditating, hold the crystal of your choosing in your hand or close to your heart. Use its energy and power to achieve your goals, no matter what they are.

Share the Wonder of Animals

A s an emotional and intuitive sign, Pisces often has a gift when it comes to animals. In fact, some people believe you can communicate with animals on a deeper level. Pisces's compassionate soul also finds sharing with others very rewarding. As a Pisces, your gentle spirit works especially well with children, so impart your bond with animals on a child! Whether you take them to a petting zoo or nearby farm or spend time with animals in a shelter, it will be an invaluable experience for both of you.

Explore Your Artistic Side

―――――――――

Water signs are instinctively very artistic. Tap into your creative side by trying a new craft, such as watercolor painting. Watercolors are a more forgiving medium for novice painters than oil paints. Try painting ocean scenes, waterfalls, or lakes. The act of painting can be very soothing for the artist. If you are struggling at first, you may find it helps to look at an image to replicate as you paint, or purchase an acrylic paint-by-numbers kit. Once you've gotten the hang of brushstrokes and color blending, you can create an original piece.

Use a Mantra

Caring Pisces values deep relationships with those around her. When she feels disconnected from a loved one, it creates an imbalance that leaves her unsure. This feeling of instability can cause Pisces to flee to the metaphysical world and avoid communication with others altogether. Fortunately, you can ground yourself and gain back confidence in your relationships by reciting a special mantra.

A mantra is a unique phrase that you repeat out loud in order to center yourself and tune out unhelpful thoughts. A great mantra for Pisces is "Love and compassion will help us all." Use this mantra to steady yourself and prevent that urge to flee when you feel uncertain of a current relationship.

Show Off Another Time Period

I f you love a particular historical period, consider decorating part of your home with objects from that era. Because of their empathetic abilities, water signs are able to build worlds in their minds that they can visit every now and again. Bridge the gap between your reality and imagination by surrounding yourself with objects that remind you of another time and place. You could create an American Civil War room, an ancient Egyptian room, or a Viking room.

If you are more in love with a certain place than a time period, apply the same principle. Collect objects from that area and put them on display.

Affirm Your Instincts

―――――――

Pisces has a special gift of insight that those around her admire. But sometimes unexpected things happen, regardless of how vigilant she is in reading situations. These bumps in the road can cause Pisces to doubt her intuition. If you feel that self-doubt creeping in, you can give yourself a much-needed confidence boost through the use of an affirmation. An affirmation, written down and revisited as needed, will serve as a reminder of your abilities.

The perfect affirmation for Pisces is "I trust in my intuition, and incorporate it in my daily life." There is a reason people often say Pisces has a sixth sense. But even the most insightful are not responsible for predicting every turn life takes you through. This doesn't mean your intuition is wrong and you should stop listening to it, so use your affirmation as a reminder of that fact.

Hone Your Photography Skills

———————

As a water sign, you have incredible observation skills and an eye for beauty. This makes you the ideal photographer. You are able to identify poignancy in any scene, and isolate it with the perfect shot. You also love to keep copies of all the photographs you take so you can revisit these moments whenever you want.

To enhance your photography skills, consider investing in a high-quality camera with digital capabilities. This way you can have a digital record of your work, in addition to prints. Before you purchase, do some research to find out which camera will be best for you and your skill level.

Pin a Guardian Angel
to Your Collar

———————————

As a sign connected to the psyche, Pisces is tuned in to the powers that be. This includes the intangible forces and past people who may be watching over you throughout your life, offering guidance and aid. Pin an angel to your coat collar or carry it with you in your bag or car as a reminder that you are not alone in your journey. There is protection, guidance, and support waiting for you whenever you may need it.

Pamper Yourself

———————

Pampering yourself is essential for any self-care routine. For water signs this means spending time focusing on their outer appearance as well as their inner wellness. Dedicate time to indulging yourself with a spa facial. Facials are great for increasing circulation in your facial muscles and hydrating the skin. They can also decrease puffiness and slow the formation of wrinkles.

If you don't have the budget to pay for a spa-level facial, you can always try at-home masks. Many of these masks are made from ingredients that are already in your pantry or refrigerator, such as cucumber. Research which kind of mask will work best for your skin type.

Grow a Bonsai Tree

Creative and nurturing Pisces loves helping things grow and flourish in beautiful ways. Grow a bonsai tree! This miniature, eye-catching plant is the perfect hobby for exercising both your artistic and caring sides. Bonsai trees are also a part of feng shui, which uses nature and placement to bring balance and positive chi to your home. You can find bonsai kits online, as well as in many garden centers. Be sure to follow instructions on care, and invest in a small pair of scissors for shaping your tree as it grows.

Flavor Your Water

You already know that drinking enough water is one key to good health, but this is especially true for water signs. You need to ingest enough water every day to keep your body strong. Staying hydrated doesn't have to be boring, though. Hydrating with water is by far the best option, but you can spice things up by adding a few ingredients to make your own flavored water. Try stirring in a few strawberries or raspberries, or just add a splash of lemon juice or cucumbers to your water pitcher. Not only do these ingredients brighten the flavor of your water, but many of them have antioxidant properties that can boost your immune system.

See *The Little Mermaid*

The mermaid is Pisces's finny sister. And not just because they are both linked to the element of water. In fact, though Pisces lives in the physical world, she is often compared to this mythical being, due to her misty planetary ruler, Neptune. Pisces, like a mermaid, has a similarly misty allure, deep intuition, and connection to the metaphysical realm.

Visit Copenhagen, Denmark, where you can find *The Little Mermaid* statue. Made of bronze and posed on a rock along the Langelinie Pier, this special statue was created in honor of the Hans Christian Andersen fairytale. Unable to travel for a while? You can also pop in the animated movie for a burst of mystical inspiration (and childhood nostalgia).

Protect Yourself from Energy Vampires

Water signs feel deeply and can easily be drained by emotionally manipulative people. Trust your gut when it comes to whom you spend your time with. If you find that someone is particularly toxic to you or you feel that your energy is depleted after seeing them, consider removing them from your life. As a water sign, you need to care for your emotional wellness and protect yourself against energy vampires. If you are feeling particularly vulnerable, try carrying around a piece of rose quartz to buffer against negativity. Wearing the crystal as a necklace near your heart is even better.

Visit a Monastery

Ruled by Neptune, Pisces is deeply connected to the metaphysical world. Nourish your spirituality by visiting a monastery. One of the oldest types of spiritual centers in the world, a monastery is the living quarters and place of worship for a group of monks or nuns. Monasteries are part of many spiritual traditions, including Buddhism, Christianity, and Hinduism. You can visit one of thousands of beautiful monasteries across the globe, or take a quick trip to one closer to home to meditate or pray where countless individuals have before you. In Europe, some monasteries also offer inexpensive accommodation for travelers so check out the possibilities!

Write a Story

_____

Your imagination is expansive as a water sign. You have the gift of creation, seamlessly moving between reality and the made-up worlds in your mind. Some of the best writers working today are water signs, so try putting your visions down on paper and sharing them with the world. Start small by writing a short story, or even just the beginning paragraphs of a larger project. Live inside your own imagination for a while and see what comes forth. Remember that not every sentence you write needs to be perfect. Just focus on expressing your ideas, and you can go back and revise what you've already written later on.

Take Dance Lessons

A s an expressive water sign, Pisces delights in fluid movements that allow her to release her many emotions. Sign up for a dance lesson to find your own watery rhythm, and maybe work up a healthy sweat in the process.

Great dances for Pisces involve passionate movements that encourage emotional expression, and often a dance partner to share the rhythm with. Try the intimate waltz or the fast-paced tango with a partner, or move to your own inner tempo with a freestyle routine.

Volunteer

In nature inactive water becomes stagnant and attracts bacteria. Water needs to run, gurgle, babble, and sway. Water signs are the same way. Doing nothing can make a water sign feel useless and bored. To quench your desire to be active and helpful, volunteer at an organization that you care about deeply. Play with dogs at a shelter, read to children at the library, or make lunches for the homeless. For you, being active doesn't just mean moving your body; it also means spending your time meaningfully. These small acts can change the world!

Create a Home Retreat

For Pisces, the home is where she can truly be herself. As an emotional and reflective sign, she requires a lot of alone time to recharge her batteries and enjoy fun solitary hobbies such as reading and drawing. Create a special space in your home that will serve as the perfect oasis for relaxation and solitary enjoyment. This space should incorporate calming blue accents. Also be sure to add plenty of cozy seating options and blankets.

Join a Club

_____

Water signs love to be included in groups, even though they can sometimes get overwhelmed by too many people. The sense of belonging is important for them to feel appreciated and loved. The key for you as a water sign is to find a small group that focuses on something you really love. This could be a book club that meets once a month, a cooking class, or a wildlife club that goes on adventures in nature. There will be no shortage of interesting conversation; you'll find loads to talk about with people who share your loves.

Keep a Dream Diary

Water signs have notoriously vivid dreams that stick with them after waking. You may even dream of future events, or have trouble deciphering if what happened was a dream or reality.

Try keeping a dream diary to chronicle all of the dreams you remember. When you wake up and the dream is fresh in your mind, take a few minutes to write down key words that describe the dream. Ask yourself some questions: How did you feel? Who was there? What was happening? The more detail you can put on paper, the better able you'll be to interpret the dreams later on.

Adorn Your Bed with Pillows

———————

Pisces is a sign of relaxation and comfort. Nestle into soft surroundings by purchasing pillows of all sizes for your bed. Your comfy nest won't just be for sleeping, it will also be your hub for creativity and relaxing solitary hobbies.

Try to include both soft pillows for resting and firmer pillows for leaning against when enjoying some alone time. This mix of support will avoid backaches and slouched postures. Be sure to also provide a variety of enjoyable textures to your oasis, such as velvet, silk, and fleece.

People-Watch

Pisces spends a great deal of her time within her thoughts. She loves to reflect, in memories or daydreams, and it is often from these inner thoughts that she gains insights into both herself and the outside world. Feed that natural urge for thought by people-watching. People-watching is a simple pastime that involves sitting back to observe the activity of those around you, often in a bustling public space. You can take a trip to the local coffee shop for an afternoon, or spend the day at a popular park taking in all of the sights and sounds (and some nice fresh air as well).

Take a Fishing Trip

———————

Symbolized by the element of water and the Fish, Pisces shares a bond with this natural substance and its scaly inhabitants. Nourish this connection with a fishing trip! An adventure on either salt or freshwater is just the thing to rejuvenate Pisces. The waves will feel like a second home as she seeks out her astrological symbol. Make it a full-day affair by packing a delicious lunch and bringing along a book or other relaxing activity to pass the time as you fish. How many types of fish can you spot?

Buy a Witch's Hat

Mystical Pisces has an affinity for all things supernatural, including witchcraft. In fact, it is often believed that Pisces exists in two realms at once: the material and the metaphysical. This is represented by her astrological symbol of two fish tied together, swimming in opposite directions.

Tap into your magical side by buying a witch's hat (or full costume!). In need of some inspiration, or perhaps a reminder of your abilities? Put on your hat and feel the divine powers of the witch course through you. You may even be compelled to cast a spell or two.

Start a Collection

Since water signs feel at home near bodies of water, it makes sense for them to pick up pieces of those water sources with them wherever they go. Start collecting stones, rocks, or shells from every body of water you visit. The energy of the water will stay within these objects and help keep you balanced when you are on dry land. When you are feeling lost, sit quietly and hold each object in your hands. Feel the positive vibrations radiating from them. If you'd like, you can create an altar of your water objects in your bedroom to help attract calm thoughts while you drift off to dreamland. Or, when you are in need of an energy boost, put one in your purse or pocket so you can hold it whenever you want as you go about your day.

Sing While You Work

As a daydreamer, Pisces can sometimes be tempted to delay boring chores for a far more exciting trip through her imagination. Due to her sensitive nature, she may also become stressed if there are a lot of things on her to-do list. But who doesn't struggle through chores from time to time? Everyone has a least favorite task or two that feels unpleasant and sometimes difficult to finish, whether it's sorting through bills or deep-cleaning your home for guests.

Use your love of music to stay motivated. Humming, whistling, or even belting out a tune while completing your everyday tasks will keep you relaxed and help you tackle even the least pleasant chores with ease.

About the Author

Constance Stellas is an astrologer of Greek heritage with more than twenty-five years of experience. She primarily practices in New York City and counsels a variety of clients, including business CEOs, artists, and scholars. She has been interviewed by *The New York Times*, *Marie Claire*, and *Working Woman*, and has appeared on several New York TV morning shows, featuring regularly on Sirius XM and other national radio programs as well. Constance is the astrologer for *HuffPost* and a regular contributor to Thrive Global. She is also the author of several titles, including *The Astrology Gift Guide*, *Advanced Astrology for Life*, *The Everything® Sex Signs Book*, and the graphic novel series Tree of Keys, as well as coauthor of *The Hidden Power of Everyday Things*. Learn more about Constance at her website, ConstanceStellas.com, or on *Twitter* (@Stellastarguide).